Don't Get Angry, Annie

Stay Calm

Lisa Regan

Enslow Publishing
101 W. 23rd Street
Suite 240
New York, NY 10011
USA

enslow.com

It might be useful for parents or teachers to read our "How to use this book" guide on pages 28–29 before looking at Annie's dilemmas. The points for discussion on these pages are helpful to share with your child once you have read the book together.

This edition published in 2018 by Enslow Publishing, LLC.
101 W. 23rd Street, Suite 240, New York, NY 10011

Copyright © 2018 Wayland, a division of Hachette Children's Group

Cataloging-in-Publication Data

Names: Regan, Lisa.
Title: Don't get angry, Annie: stay calm / Lisa Regan.
Description: New York : Enslow Publishing, 2018. | Series: You choose | Includes index.
Identifiers: ISBN 9780766088849 (pbk.) | ISBN 9780766087002 (library bound) | ISBN 9780766088801 (6 pack)
Subjects: LCSH: Anger—Juvenile literature. | Self-control—Juvenile literature.
Classification: LCC BF575.A5 R44 2018 | DDC 152.4'7—dc23

Printed in the United States of America

Illustrations by Lucy Neale

Contents

Hello, Annie!

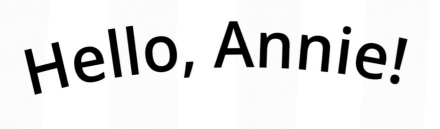

Annie is **kind**. But sometimes she feels **angry**. When things don't work out quite right, Annie starts to feel really **annoyed**.

Follow Annie as she finds herself in tricky situations in which she must learn how to stay **calm**.

YOU choose too!

Play together, Annie

Annie's best friend, Rosie, is playing with Jamelia. Annie wishes Rosie was playing with her instead.

Annie can feel herself getting **annoyed.**

What should Annie choose to do?

Should Annie:

a push Jamelia away and play with Rosie instead?

b ask if she can play, too?

c take all their toys away?

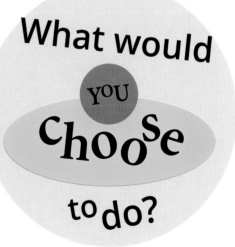

Annie, choose **b**

Friends shouldn't get annoyed if their friends play with other people. It's okay to have lots of different **playmates**. The important thing is to be nice so that they still want you as their friend, too.

What would **YOU** **Choose** to do?

Don't spoil it, Annie

Annie is trying to draw a
dog, but she doesn't think
her drawing is very good.

Annie is getting **angry** with herself and with the picture.

What should Annie choose to do?

Should Annie:

a crush the paper into a ball and throw it across the room?

b scribble on it until she feels better?

C start a new drawing and try really hard to get it right?

Annie, choose **C**

You may not get everything right the very first time! Take a deep breath and try again. Your work will be better if you stay calm, rather than getting angry.

What would YOU choose to do?

Do as Mom says, Annie

Annie wants a cookie.
They look so yummy!

Her mom says Annie can't have a cookie because it is almost time for her dinner.

What should Annie choose to do?

Should Annie:

a go and play until dinner is ready?

b **secretly** take a cookie when Mom isn't looking?

c get angry and shout that it's not fair?

Annie, choose **a**

Grown-ups usually have a good reason for saying no. Sometimes moms and dads do know best! Try to listen to them and do what they say without getting angry.

What would **YOU** choose to do?

Be kind, Annie

Annie's little brother is **spoiling** her game. He's moving the pieces the wrong way.

Annie thinks he's too young to play **properly**.

What should Annie choose to do?

Should Annie:

a scream at him that he **ruins** all her fun?

b push him over and run off to play in her room?

C make up an easier game so that her brother can join in?

Annie, choose **C**

When you were little, some things were hard for you, too. If you're feeling mad, count to 10 quietly. By then your anger should have started to go away.

What would **YOU** choose to do?

Stay calm, Annie

The teacher tells Annie off for talking in class.

Annie feels so **angry** – she wasn't the only one talking!

What should Annie choose to do?

Should Annie:

a make a big **fuss** and shout in front of the whole class?

b pinch the other children who got her into trouble?

C stay quiet for the rest of the lesson so she doesn't get told off again?

Annie, choose **C**

It's hard to stay calm when you are told off for something that other people were doing wrong, too. You can't change what has happened, but you can make sure you do the right thing next time.

What would **YOU** choose to do?

Well done, Annie!

Hey, look at Annie!
Now that she can stay calm,
she's feeling much
happier.

Did you choose the right thing to do? If you did, big cheers for you!

If you chose some of the other answers, try to think about Annie's choices so you can stop yourself from getting mad next time. Then it will be big smiles all round!

And remember— don't get angry, stay calm!

How to use this book

This book can be used by an adult and a child together. It is based on common situations that pose a challenge to all children. Invite your child to talk about each of the choices. Ask questions such as "Why do you think Annie should play with both Rosie and Jamelia?"

Discuss the wrong choices, as well as the right ones, with your child. Describe what is happening in the following pictures and talk about what the wrong and right choices might be.

• Don't get mad because you're told not to do something. Adults have good reasons for their rules.
• It's okay to feel angry

sometimes, but it isn't okay to take it out on others. Hurting people is wrong.

• Think about why other people do what they do, instead of getting angry with them.

• Don't destroy things if you feel angry. That will make you angrier!

Ask your child to imagine things that make them feel angry. Explain to them that it's okay to feel mad about some of these things. Tell them anger is a normal feeling for people to have, but let them know that they must learn to show their anger in a healthy way.

Talk about how showing anger by hitting or shouting can make people hurt others or spoil things. Show your child how they can express their anger in a healthy way by telling others how they feel. Explain how good it feels to be in charge of the way you behave!

Glossary

calm Not angry.

fuss Bad behavior such as shouting or complaining.

kind Able to think about other people and their feelings.

playmates Friends to play with.

properly In the right way, correctly.

ruins Spoiling something or breaking it.

secretly Doing or saying something in private, so no one else knows about what you are doing or saying.

spoiling Destroying something.

Index

Titles in the series

 Like all children, Annie sometimes gets really, really angry! She has lots of choices to make—but which are the CALM ones?

 Like all children, Carlos sometimes does things that are wrong and doesn't come clean. He has lots of choices to make—but which are the TRUTHFUL ones?

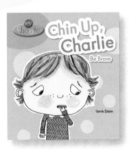 Like all children, Charlie sometimes feels a little scared. He has lots of choices to make—but which are the BRAVE ones?

 Like all children, Gertie sometimes plays a little dirty. She has lots of choices to make—but which are the FAIR ones?

 Like all children, Harry sometimes takes things that don't belong to him. He has lots of choices to make—but which are the HONEST ones?

 Like all children, Henry sometimes gets angry and sometimes he hits, too. He has lots of choices to make—but which are the GENTLE ones?

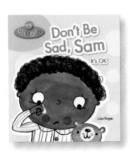 Like all children, Sam sometimes feels sad, and he doesn't know how to make himself feel better. He has lots of choices to make—but which are the HAPPY ones?

 Like all children, Tilly wants to do everything right now, and sometimes she just can't wait! She has lots of choices to make—but which are the PATIENT ones?